Beginner Biography

Jim Thorpe
World's Greatest Athlete

by Jennifer Marino Walters
illustrated by Scott R. Brooks

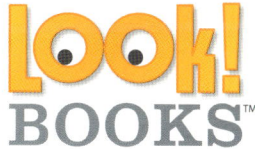

Red Chair Press   Egremont, Massachusetts

Look! Books are produced and published by Red Chair Press:
Red Chair Press LLC   PO Box 333   South Egremont, MA 01258-0333
www.redchairpress.com

 FREE lesson guide at www.redchairpress.com/free-activities

Publisher's Cataloging-In-Publication Data
(Provided by Cassidy Cataloguing Services, Inc.)
Names: Marino Walters, Jennifer, author. | Brooks, Scott R., illustrator.
Title: Jim Thorpe : world's greatest athlete / by Jennifer Marino Walters ; illustrated by Scott R. Brooks.

Other titles: Look! books (Red Chair Press). Beginner biography

Description: Egremont, Massachusetts : Red Chair Press, [2024] | Includes index. | Interest age level: 006-009. | Summary: Jim Thorpe, a Native American born in Oklahoma, played pro baseball in New York, Cincinnati, and Boston but he was an even better football player. In the 1912 Olympic Games, he won gold medals in the decathlon and pentathlon events proving his athletic talents.--Publisher.

Identifiers: ISBN: 9781643712529 (library hardcover) | 9781643712581 (softcover) | 9781643712642 (ebook) | LCCN: 2022943802

Subjects: LCSH: Thorpe, Jim, 1887-1953--Juvenile literature. | Indian athletes--United States-- Biography--Juvenile literature. | Professional athletes--United States--Biography--Juvenile literature. | Olympic athletes--United States--Biography--Juvenile literature. | CYAC: Thorpe, Jim, 1887-1953. | Indian athletes--United States--Biography. | Professional athletes--United States--Biography. | Olympic athletes--United States--Biography. | LCGFT: Biographies. | BISAC: JUVENILE NONFICTION / Biography & Autobiography / Cultural, Ethnic & Regional. | JUVENILE NONFICTION / People & Places / United States / Native American. | JUVENILE NONFICTION / Sports & Recreation / Track & Field.

Classification: LCC: GV697.T5 M37 2024 | DDC: 796/.092--dc23

Copyright © 2025 Red Chair Press LLC
RED CHAIR PRESS, the RED CHAIR and associated logos are registered trademarks of Red Chair Press LLC.

All rights reserved. No part of this book may be reproduced, stored in an information or retrieval system, or transmitted in any form by any means, electronic, mechanical including photocopying, recording, or otherwise without the prior written permission from the Publisher. For permissions, contact info@redchairpress.com

Photo credits: Library of Congress

Printed in the United States of America

0324 1P F24CG

Table of Contents

Bright Path 4

Star Athlete 6

Olympic History 8

Professional Sports 12

Later Struggles 14

The Greatest Athlete 16

Big Honors 18

A Legacy Restored 20

Big Dates in Jim's Life 22

Words to Know 23

Learn More at the Library 23

Index 24

Bright Path

On May 28, 1887, Jim Thorpe was born in Indian Territory, now Oklahoma. Jim's parents were Sac and Fox Indians. They gave him the name Wa-Tho-Huk, which meant "Bright Path."

Good to Know

Because official records weren't kept at the time, some people say Thorpe and his twin brother Charlie were born in 1888, not 1887.

Jim began to **forge** a bright path while attending the Carlisle Indian Industrial School in Pennsylvania. One day in 1907, he joined a track-and-field practice on campus and broke the school's high-jump record.

Star Athlete

Jim soon became a track star at Carlisle. He also played on the school's baseball, hockey, and lacrosse teams. He even won a ballroom dancing championship.

Jim was a star athlete for Coach "Pop" Warner at Carlisle Indian School.

Good to Know

At Carlisle, Jim played football against future U.S. President Dwight Eisenhower, who said of Jim, "He could do everything anybody else could do—and do it better."

But Jim really shined at football. He led the Carlisle team to an incredible record of 23 wins, two losses, and one tie in the 1911 and 1912 seasons. The wins included a victory over top-ranked Harvard in 1911 as well as a big win over West Point in 1912. Jim received All-American honors both years.

Olympic History

In 1912, Jim became part of the U.S. track-and-field team at the Olympic Games in Sweden. First, he won gold in the **pentathlon**, a 5-sport event. That made him the first Native American to win an Olympic gold medal for the United States.

A week later, Jim's shoes went missing during the three-day **decathlon**. His coach put together a pair of mismatched shoes for him. Jim still won the gold medal and set records in several events. His record in the 1,500-meter run went unbeaten until 1972.

Good to Know

When King Gustaf V of Sweden placed the gold medals around Jim's neck, he called Jim "the greatest athlete in the world."

But in January 1913, the International Olympic Committee (IOC) learned that Jim had played minor-league baseball in 1909 and 1910. Getting paid to play a sport broke the rules of **amateur** competition. The committee took away Jim's gold medals and removed his scores from the official record.

Good to Know

Jim received 8,412.95 points out of a possible 10,000 in the decathlon. He beat the runner-up, Sweden's Hugo Wieslander, by 688 points.

Professional Sports

Despite the disappointment, Jim continued to play sports. He joined Major League Baseball in 1913 and played six seasons with the New York Giants, Cincinnati Reds, and Boston Braves. He had only average success as a major league ballplayer.

Jim with the NY Giants in 1913

Jim did much better playing professional football. He signed with the Canton, Ohio, Bulldogs in 1915 and led the team to championships in 1916, 1917, and 1919. In 1920, the Bulldogs and 13 other teams formed the American Professional Football Association. That soon became the National Football League (NFL), and Jim served as the league's first president.

Later Struggles

Jim remained in the NFL until 1928, playing with several teams over 12 seasons. From 1922–1923, he also coached and played for an all-Native American team called the Oorang Indians.

But after Jim's sports career ended, he struggled to support his seven children. He even tried acting, appearing in more than 60 films from 1931 to 1950. But most of his roles were very small parts. He also worked as a security guard, a construction worker, and more.

The Greatest Athlete

Despite his struggles, Jim worked hard to help Native Americans. He started a casting company to help get film roles for Native Americans. He also gave speeches about his life.

But no one forgot Jim's athletic success. In 1950, the Associated Press (a news organization) named him the greatest athlete of the first half of the 20th century.

Big Honors

On March 28, 1953, Jim died of a heart attack. But he continued to receive honors. In 1954, two small Pennsylvania towns combined and renamed themselves "Jim Thorpe, PA." Jim's body remains buried there even though one of his sons tried to have his body moved back to Oklahoma for burial.

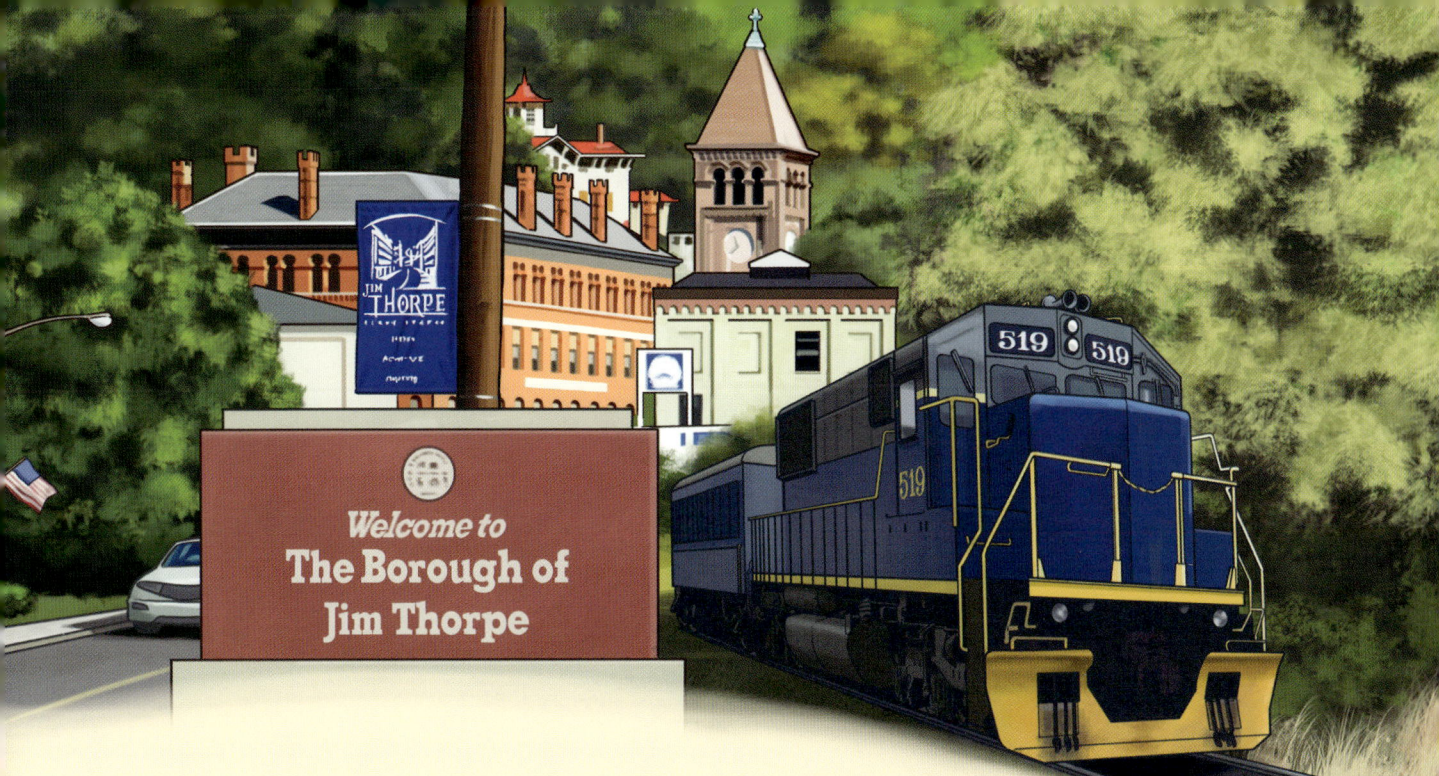

In 1963, Jim was elected one of the first members of the Pro Football Hall of Fame. He is also part of the College Football, National Track and Field, and U.S. Olympic Halls of Fame.

A Legacy Restored

Jim's family never stopped fighting for his Olympic wins to be recognized. In 1982, the IOC re-named him a co-champion of the pentathlon and decathlon. His family received **replica** gold medals in January 1983.

In July 2022, the IOC finally re-named Jim the sole winner of the 1912 Olympic pentathlon and decathlon and returned his scores to the record books. After 110 years, Jim Thorpe's Olympic **legacy** and his honor were restored.

Good to Know

In 2000, an ABC Wide World of Sports Internet poll voted Jim as the greatest athlete of the 20th century.

Timeline: Big Dates in Jim's Life

1887: Jim is born in present-day central Oklahoma.

1912: Jim wins gold medals in the pentathlon and decathlon at the Olympic Games.

1913: The International Olympic Committee (IOC) takes away Jim's gold medals after learning he had played semi-professional baseball.

1915: Jim signs on to play professional football with the Canton Bulldogs, leading the team to championships in 1916, 1917, and 1919.

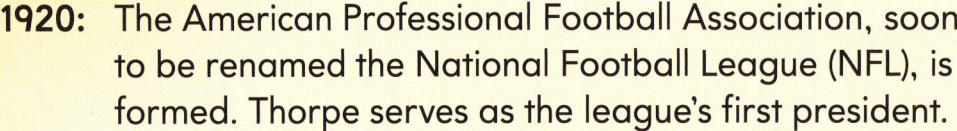

1920: The American Professional Football Association, soon to be renamed the National Football League (NFL), is formed. Thorpe serves as the league's first president.

1950: The Associated Press names Jim the greatest athlete of the first half of the 20th century.

1953: Jim dies of a heart attack at age 64 at his home in Lomita, California.

1954: Two small Pennsylvania towns merge to become Jim Thorpe, PA. Jim's body is buried there.

1982: The IOC re-names Jim as a co-champion of the 1912 Olympic pentathlon and decathlon.

2022: Jim is officially re-named the sole winner of the 1912 Olympic pentathlon and decathlon.

Words to Know

amateur: done for enjoyment and not as a paid job

decathlon: an athletic contest that includes ten different events (deca means ten in Greek)

forge: to form or create something

legacy: something that comes from someone in the past

pentathlon: an athletic contest that includes five different events

replica: an exact or very close copy of something

Learn More at the Library

(Check out these books to read with others)

Buckley Jr, James. *Who Was Jim Thorpe?* Penguin Workshop, 2023.

Bruchac, Joseph. *Jim Thorpe's Bright Path.* Lee & Low Books, 2008.

Coulson, Art. *Unstoppable: How Jim Thorpe and the Carlisle Indian School Football Team Defeated Army.* Capstone Editions, 2018.

Labrecque, Ellen. *Jim Thorpe: An Athlete for the Ages.* Union Square Kids, 2010.

Index

Canton, OH, Bulldogs 13
football 7
Hall of Fame 19
Major League Baseball (MLB) 12
National Football League (NFL) 13
Oklahoma 4, 18
Olympics (IOC) 8, 10, 20–21
Oorang Indians 14
Pennsylvania 5, 18
Sac and Fox 4
track-and-field 5, 8

About the Author

Jennifer Marino Walters is the author of 20 books for children. She lives with her husband and their twin boys and daughter in the Washington, D.C. area. When she's not writing, you can find her cheering on her three little athletes at the local baseball and softball fields.